U.S. Department of Justice
Office of Justice Programs
810 Seventh Street NW.
Washington, DC 20531

I0473152

Eric H. Holder, Jr.
U.S. Attorney General

Laurie O. Robinson
Assistant Attorney General

Jeff Slowikowski
Acting Administrator
Office of Juvenile Justice and Delinquency Prevention

Office of Justice Programs
Innovation • Partnerships • Safer Neighborhoods
www.ojp.usdoj.gov

Office of Juvenile Justice and Delinquency Prevention
ojjdp.gov

This document was prepared by Fox Valley Technical College under cooperative agreement number 2009–MC–CX–K058 from the Office of Juvenile Justice and Delinquency Prevention (OJJDP), Office of Justice Programs, U.S. Department of Justice.

Points of view or opinions expressed in this document are those of the authors and do not necessarily represent the official positions or policies of OJJDP or the U.S. Department of Justice.

The Office of Juvenile Justice and Delinquency Prevention is a component of the Office of Justice Programs, which also includes the Bureau of Justice Assistance; the Bureau of Justice Statistics; the Community Capacity Development Office; the National Institute of Justice; the Office for Victims of Crime; and the Office of Sex Offender Sentencing, Monitoring, Apprehending, Registering, and Tracking (SMART).

Federal Resources on

Missing and Exploited Children

A Directory for Law Enforcement and Other Public and Private Agencies

Federal Agency Task Force for Missing and Exploited Children

Sixth Edition
2011

Federal Agency Task Force for
Missing and Exploited Children

U.S. Department of Defense
Family Advocacy Program
DOD Representative to the National Center for Missing & Exploited Children

U.S. Department of Education
Office of Safe and Drug-Free Schools

U.S. Department of Health and Human Services
Administration on Children, Youth and Families – Family and Youth Services Bureau
Administration on Children, Youth and Families – Children's Bureau –
Office on Child Abuse and Neglect

U.S. Department of Homeland Security
U.S. Immigration and Customs Enforcement
U.S. Secret Service – Forensic Services Division

U.S. Department of Justice
Child Exploitation and Obscenity Section
FBI – Behavioral Analysis Unit
FBI – Crimes Against Children Unit
FBI – Innocent Images Unit
INTERPOL-Washington, U.S. National Central Bureau
Office for Victims of Crime
Office of Juvenile Justice and Delinquency Prevention

U.S. Department of State
Bureau of Consular Affairs – Office of Children's Issues

U.S. Postal Service
U.S. Postal Inspection Service

Association of Missing and Exploited Children's Organizations, Inc.

National Center for Missing & Exploited Children

Acknowledgments

Compiling this directory required the commitment, dedication, and cooperation of many agencies and organizations and persons within those agencies. The Federal Agency Task Force wishes to thank the following individuals who generously gave their time and energy to the revised version of the *Federal Resources on Missing and Exploited Children Directory*.

Eve Birge
Office of Safe and Drug-Free Schools
U.S. Department of Education

Michael Blewett
Family Advocacy Program
U.S. Department of Defense

Mary Ann Brewster
INTERPOL-Washington, U.S. National Central
 Bureau
U.S. Department of Justice

Ben Ermini
National Center for Missing & Exploited Children

Rachel Selina Evans
INTERPOL-Washington, U.S. National Central
 Bureau
U.S. Department of Justice

Michelle Ford-Stepney
INTERPOL-Washington, U.S. National Central
 Bureau
U.S. Department of Justice

Margery Gehan
Office of Children's Issues
Bureau of Consular Affairs
U.S. Department of State

Alexandra Gelber
Child Exploitation and Obscenity Section
U.S. Department of Justice

Lisa Holman
U.S. Postal Inspection Service
U.S. Postal Service

Christopher Johnson
Crimes Against Children Unit
Federal Bureau of Investigation
U.S. Department of Justice

Wendy Jolley-Kabi
Association of Missing and Exploited Children's
 Organizations, Inc.

Ron Laney
Child Protection Division
Office of Juvenile Justice and Delinquency
 Prevention
U.S. Department of Justice

Catherine Luby
Office on Child Abuse and Neglect
Children's Bureau
Administration on Children, Youth and Families
Administration for Children and Families
U.S. Department of Health and Human Services

Marianna Novielli
Forensic Services Division
U.S. Secret Service
U.S. Department of Homeland Security

Eric Pond
U.S. Immigration and Customs Enforcement
U.S. Department of Homeland Security

Barbara Robertson
Terrorism and International Victim Assistance
 Services Division
Office for Victims of Crime
U.S. Department of Justice

Nicholas Savage
Innocent Images Unit
Federal Bureau of Investigation
U.S. Department of Justice

Eric Trest
Naval Criminal Investigative Service
U.S. Department of Defense

LeBretia White
Family and Youth Services Bureau
Administration on Children, Youth and Families
Administration for Children and Families
U.S. Department of Health and Human Services

Contents

FEDERAL AGENCIES

U.S. Department of Defense

U.S. Department of Education

U.S. Department of Health and Human Services

U.S. Department of Homeland Security

U.S. Department of Justice

NON-FEDERAL AGENCIES

Introduction

The Federal Agency Task Force for Missing and Exploited Children was created in 1995, by then Attorney General Janet Reno to coordinate Federal resources and services to effectively address the needs of missing, abducted, and exploited children and their families. The mission of the Task Force is to (1) advocate for missing and exploited children and their families, (2) initiate positive change to enhance services and resources for missing and exploited children, their families, and the agencies and organizations that serve them, (3) promote communication and cooperation among agencies and organizations at the Federal level, and (4) serve as the focal point for coordination of services and resources.

The Task Force includes representatives from 16 Federal agencies and 2 non-Federal agencies that work directly with cases involving missing and exploited children and their families. The term "missing child," as used in this *Directory*, refers to any youth whose whereabouts are unknown to his or her legal guardian. This includes children who have been abducted or kidnapped by a family or a nonfamily member, a child who is a throw away, or a child who is otherwise missing. The term "child exploitation" refers to any youth under the age of 18 who has been exploited or victimized for profit or personal advantage, which includes children who are victims of pornography, prostitution, sexual tourism, trafficking, and sexual abuse. These missing and exploited cases include both national and international cases.

First published in 1996, the *Federal Resources on Missing and Exploited Children's Directory* has become an effective resource that can be used by agencies and organizations involved in the safe recovery of missing children. The *Directory* contains the most up-to-date information on and links to other agencies and organizations that can help in finding a solution. The *Directory* is a compilation of the many services, programs, publications, and training that address issues of child sexual exploitation, child pornography, child abduction, and missing children cases. It describes the role of each Federal Task Force member agency in the location and recovery of missing and exploited children, the types of services and support that are available, the various methods for accessing these services, and additional resources.

This new edition of the *Directory* has been redesigned to provide comprehensive, accessible agency and organization information in a concise, user-friendly format. It will be an indispensable tool for practitioners dealing with the many challenges of returning children safely.

Federal Agencies

U.S. Department of Defense
DOD Representative to the National Center for Missing & Exploited Children

The Naval Criminal Investigative Service (NCIS), U.S. Army Criminal Investigation Command (USACIDC), Air Force Office of Special Investigations (AFOSI), and Coast Guard Investigative Service (CGIS) have created a Department of Defense (DOD) position at the National Center for Missing & Exploited Children (NCMEC). The DOD representative primarily serves as liaison to the Missing and Exploited Children Divisions at NCMEC, assisting with the Child Victim Identification Program and the CyberTipline. The DOD representative also assists law enforcement agencies with DOD support as it relates to child exploitation investigations.

Services offered in these fields:

- Technical assistance
- Out-of-house training
- Criminal investigation

Assistance provided in these areas:

- Child abduction
- Parental abduction and kidnapping
- International abduction and kidnapping
- Human trafficking
- Runaway children
- Child sexual exploitation
- Child prostitution
- Child pornography
- Sex tourism
- Internet crimes
- Military resources

Services provided to the following:

- Federal, State, and local agencies

Contact Info

National Center for Missing & Exploited Children
699 Prince Street
Alexandria, VA 22314
Attn: DOD Representative

tel 703–778–6480

fax 703–224–2131

email mcio@ncmec.org

U.S. Department of Defense
Family Advocacy Law Enforcement Training

The Family Advocacy Law Enforcement Training (FALET) program provides comprehensive training, direct unit support, and consultation programs in the prevention and investigation of child abuse, gang violence, and juvenile delinquency; critical incident peer support; trafficking in persons investigations; sexual assault response and investigations; and inquiries involving spouse abuse and all other forms of family violence.

Services offered in these fields:

- In-house training

Assistance provided in these areas:

- Human trafficking
- Child abduction
- Child sexual exploitation
- Child prostitution
- Child pornography
- Internet crimes
- Forensic sciences

Services provided to the following:

- Federal, State, and local agencies
- Community organizations

Contact Info

401 Manscen Loop
Suite 1721, Thurman Hall
Fort Leonard Wood, MO 65473

tel 573–563–7865

fax 573–563–8062

CONFERENCES, WORKSHOPS, AND TRAININGS

Child Abuse Prevention and Investigative Techniques Course (CAPIT)
CAPIT is an 8-day course taught in residence or by mobile training team. The course provides advanced training to selected DOD and civilian criminal investigators in the investigation of child abuse. Legal, medical, and mental health professionals, as well as victim advocates, are encouraged to attend. CAPIT focuses on the conduct of interviews, gathering of physical evidence, sensitivity to the needs of victims and nonoffending parents, and special legal considerations as they pertain to the investigation of child abuse. Child interviews, child abuse crime scenes, and psychological aspects of victims and offenders are also discussed. The role of the investigator as part of a multidisciplinary family advocacy team is emphasized.

Domestic Violence Intervention Training (DVIT)
DVIT is a 5-day multidisciplinary course taught in residence or by mobile training team. The

course provides advanced training to law enforcement domestic violence first responders. Legal, medical, and mental health professionals, as well as victim advocates, are encouraged to attend. DVIT focuses on effective intervention in and investigation of dysfunctional family incidents, with emphasis on protection of the victim and return of the family to a healthy state. Topics include multidisciplinary aspects of interventions, response techniques, dynamics of domestic violence, psychological characteristics of victims and abusers, domestic violence crime scenes, and strategies for assessing and calming domestic violence situations.

U.S. Department of Education
Office of Safe and Drug-Free Schools

The Office of Safe and Drug-Free Schools (OSDFS) provides funds and technical assistance to States, schools, and communities for programs that promote the health and well-being of students in elementary schools, secondary schools, and institutions of higher education. OSDFS programs emphasize positive, disciplined, high-achieving schools; strong parent and community involvement; effective school planning and preparedness; research-based prevention and education strategies; and the effective use of data by schools and States to select and improve high-quality programs and activities.

Services offered in these fields:

- Information dissemination and awareness raising
- Public education
- Publication support

Assistance provided in these areas:

- Human trafficking
- Child sexual exploitation
- Teen dating violence
- Internet crimes
- Reference and referral resource information

Services provided to the following:

- Federal and State agencies
- General public

Contact Info

Potomac Center Plaza
550 12th Street SW., 10066
Washington, DC 20202–6450

tel 202–245–7896

fax 202–245–7166

CONFERENCES, WORKSHOPS, AND TRAININGS

Biannual-National OSDFS Conference

http://www.osdfsnationalconference.com/conferenceinfo.aspx

RESOURCES

Human Trafficking of Children in the United States: A Fact Sheet for Schools

http://www2.ed.gov/about/offices/list/osdfs/factsheet.pdf

U.S. Department of Health and Human Services
Administration for Children and Families
Administration on Children, Youth and Families
Family and Youth Services Bureau

The Family and Youth Services Bureau (FYSB) provides national leadership on youth and family issues. The Bureau promotes positive outcomes for children, youth, and families by supporting a wide range of comprehensive services and collaborations at the local, State, tribal, and national levels.

Services offered in these fields:

- Funding and grants

Assistance provided in these areas:

- Runaway children
- Child sexual exploitation
- Teen dating violence
- Reference and referral resource information

Services provided to the following:

- Federal, State, and local agencies
- Community organizations
- Legislative and policy groups
- General public

Contact Info

1250 Maryland Avenue SW.
Washington, DC 20024

tel 202–205–8102
fax 202–205–9535

FYSB PROGRAMS

Division of Youth Services
Mentoring Children of Prisoners Program.
As many as two million young people in the United States have at least one parent behind bars. The Mentoring Children of Prisoners Program provides these often displaced and traumatized young people with opportunities to develop both a trusting relationship with a supportive, caring adult and a stable environment that can promote healthy values and strong families.

http://www.acf.hhs.gov/programs/fysb/index.htm

Runaway and Homeless Youth Program.
Each year, thousands of youth in this country run away from home, are asked to leave their homes, or become homeless. Through the Runaway and Homeless Youth Program, FYSB funds street outreach, short-term shelter, longer term transitional living, and maternity group-home programs that serve and protect young people.

Family Violence Prevention and Services Act (FVPSA)

FVPSA is the primary Federal funding stream dedicated to the support of emergency shelter and related assistance for victims of domestic violence and their dependents. Funding to tribes, States, and the territories provides core support to more than 1,500 community-based domestic violence programs. Annually, these local programs respond to more than 1.4 million calls to crisis hotlines and provide emergency shelter and other services to more than 119,000 victims of domestic violence and 120,000 children.

http://www.acf.hhs.gov/programs/fysb/index.htm

RESOURCES

National Clearinghouse on Families and Youth

http://ncfy.acf.hhs.gov/

National Domestic Violence Hotline

http://www.ndvh.org/

National Online Resource Center on Violence Against Women

http://www.vawnet.org/

National Runaway Switchboard

http://www.1800runaway.org/

Runaway and Homeless Youth Training and Technical Assistance Centers

http://www.rhyttac.ou.edu/

U.S. Department of Health and Human Services
Administration for Children and Families
Administration on Children, Youth and Families
Children's Bureau
Office on Child Abuse and Neglect

The Children's Bureau (CB) is one of two bureaus within the Administration on Children, Youth and Families, Administration for Children and Families. CB works with State and local agencies to develop programs that focus on preventing the abuse of children in troubled families, protecting children from abuse, and finding permanent placements for those who cannot safely return to their homes. One of eight teams at CB, the Office on Child Abuse and Neglect (OCAN) provides leadership and direction on the issues of child maltreatment and the prevention of abuse and neglect under the Child Abuse Prevention and Treatment Act. OCAN is the focal point for interagency collaborative efforts. The agency supports improvement in the systems that handle child abuse and neglect cases, particularly child sexual abuse and exploitation and maltreatment-related fatalities, and improvement in the investigation and prosecution of these cases through the Children's Justice Act.

Services offered in these fields:

- Grant funding
- Technical assistance
- Clearinghouse information

Assistance provided in these areas:

- Child sexual exploitation
- Child welfare

Services provided to the following:

- Federal, State, and local agencies
- Community organizations
- Legislative and policy groups
- General public

Contact Info

1250 Maryland Avenue SW.
Eighth Floor
Washington, DC 20024
tel 202–205–8618

main Web site
www.acf.hhs.gov/programs/cb/

OCAN PROGRAMS

Children's Justice Act
The Children's Justice Act provides grants to States to improve the investigation, prosecution, and judicial handling of cases of child abuse and neglect, particularly child sexual abuse and exploitation, in a manner that limits additional trauma to the child victim. This includes the handling of child fatality cases in which child abuse or neglect is suspected and some cases of children with disabilities and serious health problems who also are victims of abuse and neglect.

13

CONFERENCES, WORKSHOPS, AND TRAININGS

Children's Justice Act Information
This annual meeting is held every spring for Children's Justice Act grantees.

RESOURCES

Children's Justice Act Information

www.acf.hhs.gov/programs/cb/programs_fund/
state_tribal/justice_act.htm

Child Welfare Information Gateway
This Web site includes State child abuse reporting numbers.

www.childwelfare.gov/index.cfm

www.childwelfare.gov/pubs/relist/printer_friend
ly.cfm?rs_id=5&rate_chno=11-11172

Toll-Free Crisis Hotlines
Call Childhelp USA at 1–800–4–A–CHILD (1–800–422–4453) or find your local child protection agency listed at:

www.childwelfare.gov

U.S. Department of Homeland Security
U.S. Immigration and Customs Enforcement

U.S. Immigration and Customs Enforcement (ICE), the largest investigative arm of the U.S. Department of Homeland Security, brings a unified and coordinated focus to the enforcement of Federal immigration and customs laws. Under the auspices of the Child Exploitation Program and Operation Predator, ICE aggressively targets transborder importers, distributors, and purveyors of child exploitation materials and U.S. and foreign child sex tourists to prevent the sexual exploitation and abuse of children both in the United States and around the world. The ICE Cyber Crimes Center, Child Exploitation Section works closely with international law enforcement agencies, the Department of Justice's Child Exploitation and Obscenity Section, the U.S. Postal Inspection Service, the FBI, the Internet Crimes Against Children Regional Task Forces, and the National Center for Missing & Exploited Children (NCMEC).

ICE (under legacy U.S. Customs) was one of the first Federal law enforcement agencies to partner with NCMEC and become a point of contact for transborder tips and leads received. Today, ICE works actively on tips concerning transborder child exploitation and international child sex tourism that originate from NCMEC's toll-free hotline and Web site. ICE further develops leads from NCMEC for referral to appropriate domestic and foreign ICE field offices.

Services offered in these fields:

- Technical assistance
- In-house training
- Criminal investigation
- Prosecution
- Public education
- Publication support

Assistance provided in these areas:

- Human trafficking
- Child sexual exploitation
- Child pornography
- Sex tourism
- Internet crimes
- Forensic sciences

Services provided to the following:

- Federal, State, and local agencies
- General public

Contact Info

11320 Random Hills Road
Suite 400
Fairfax, VA 20598

tel 703–293–8005

fax 703–293–9127

main Web site
www. ce.gov

RESOURCES

ICE Field Offices
For information about ICE field offices, see:

www.ice.gov/about/investigations/contact.htm

U.S. Department of Homeland Security
U.S. Secret Service
Forensic Services Division

Under Title XXXI of the Violent Crime Control and Law Enforcement Act of 1994, the U.S. Secret Service (USSS) is mandated to provide forensic and technical assistance to the National Center for Missing & Exploited Children (NCMEC) and to State and local law enforcement authorities investigating crimes against children. In April 2003, under the Prosecuting Remedies and Tools Against the Exploitation of Children Today (PROTECT) Act, Section 322, the U.S. Secret Service statutory authority was amended. Title 18, United States Code 3056 was amended as follows: "(f) Under the direction of the Secretary of Homeland Security, officers and agents of the Secret Service are authorized, at the request of any State or local law enforcement agency, or at the request of NCMEC, to provide forensic and investigative assistance in support of any investigation involving missing and exploited children."

Since 1997, the U.S. Secret Service has provided forensic services to NCMEC in the form of polygraph examinations, handwriting and fingerprint analysis, voiceprint comparisons, audio and video enhancements, computer and other electronic media examinations, forensic photography, graphic arts, research and identification, and the Operation Safe Kid Program.

Services offered in these fields:
- Technical and forensic assistance
- Out-of-house training
- Criminal investigations
- Forensic services

Assistance provided in these areas:
- Child sexual exploitation
- Child pornography
- Internet crimes
- Forensic sciences

Services provided to the following:
- Federal, State, and local agencies
- Community organizations
- General public

Contact Info

950 H Street NW.
Suite 4200
Washington, DC 20223
ATTN: National Center for Missing &
Exploited Children Liaison

tel 202–406–5926

fax 202–406–5603

USSS PROGRAMS

(see next page)

USSS PROGRAMS

Electronic Crimes Special Agent Program

This program is comprised of special agents trained in computer forensics. Their expertise includes computer network forensics, online undercover operations, email tracing, and cellular tracking and mapping.

U.S. Secret Service
Criminal Investigative Division
950 H Street NW.
Suite 5300
Washington, DC 20223
202–406–9330

Forensic Investigative Response and Support Team (FIRST)

FIRST is comprised of forensic specialists who can respond to requests for assistance in cases involving missing and exploited children. Their expertise includes identification of fingerprints and handwriting and examination of questioned documents. Specialists are certified within their forensic disciplines and are available to provide expert testimony upon request.

Operation Safe Kids Program

Operation Safe Kids provides parents with a document that contains their child's biographical data, fingerprints, and black and white photograph. Upon request, this service is provided free of charge at special events.

Polygraph Program

The Polygraph Program is staffed by highly trained special agent examiners who use the latest technology to detect deception through the use of psycho-physiological science. Polygraph examiners are available to travel at a moment's notice with instruments that are easily transportable.

RESOURCES

USSS Field Offices

For information about USSS field offices, contact the Forensic Services Division at the U.S. Secret Service.

U.S. Department of Justice
Criminal Division
Child Exploitation and Obscenity Section

The Child Exploitation and Obscenity Section (CEOS) leads the Criminal Division's campaign against the sexual exploitation of children by investigating and prosecuting the most challenging Federal child sexual exploitation cases, launching nationwide investigations, providing guidance and training to prosecutors and agents, and shaping both domestic and international policy.

Services offered in these fields:

- Technical assistance
- In-house training
- Out-of-house training
- Criminal investigation
- Computer forensic examination and testimony
- Prosecution
- Guidance and assistance to prosecutors
- Program development and implementation
- Legislative support

Assistance provided in these areas:

- Child sexual exploitation
- Child prostitution
- Child pornography
- Child sex tourism
- Internet child exploitation crimes
- International parental abduction and kidnapping

Services provided to the following:

- Federal, State, and local agencies
- Community organizations

Contact Info
1400 New York Avenue NW.
Suite 600
Washington, DC 20530

tel 202–514–5780

fax 202–514–1793

main Web site
http://www.just ce.gov/cr m na /ceos/

U.S. Department of Justice
Federal Bureau of Investigation
Crimes Against Children Unit

The Crimes Against Children Unit (CACU) was established in 1977 to focus specifically on crimes against children. Staffed by supervisory special agents and support professionals, CACU addresses all crimes under the FBI's jurisdiction that involve the victimization of children, provides program management and fieldwide investigative oversight of critical FBI operations, and coordinates training throughout the law enforcement community. An FBI supervisory special agent is assigned full-time to the National Center for Missing & Exploited Children (NCMEC) to coordinate the use of both FBI and NCMEC resources and facilitate the most effective response to child abductions, parental kidnappings, child pornography, and other cases involving the sexual exploitation of children.

Services offered in these fields:

- Technical assistance
- Criminal investigation
- Program development and implementation
- Research and program evaluation
- Publication support

Assistance provided in these areas:

- Child abduction
- Parental abduction and kidnapping
- International abduction and kidnapping
- Runaway children
- Child sexual exploitation
- Child prostitution
- Sex tourism
- Crime prevention
- Reference and referral resource information

Services provided to the following:

- Federal, State, and local agencies

Contact Info

935 Pennsylvania Avenue NW.
Washington, DC 20535

tel 202–324–3665

fax 202–324–2731

main Web site
www.fb .gov

FBI/CACU PROGRAMS

Child Abduction Rapid Deployment (CARD) Teams

Because the first few hours after a child is abducted are critical, CACU provides a quick and effective response to all incidents of crimes against children. CACU deploys CARD teams—consisting of four to six experienced Crimes Against Children investigators who have in-depth knowledge about child abduction cases—to provide on-the-ground investigative, technical, and resource assistance to State and local law enforcement. The nationwide CARD team consists of 48 members, with two full teams serving each region of the country. CARD teams work closely with FBI Behavioral Analysis Unit representatives, National Center for the Analysis of Violent Crime Coordinators, and Crimes Against Children Coordinators.

http://www.fbi.gov/card/

Child Sex Tourism Initiative

The Child Sex Tourism Initiative addresses child sex offenders in the United States who travel abroad to procure children in other countries for sexual purposes.

http://www.fbi.gov/hq/cid/cac/crimesmain.htm

Innocence Lost National Initiative, Commercial Child Exploitation

In 2003, the FBI, in conjunction with the Department of Justice's Child Exploitation and Obscenity Section and NCMEC, launched the Innocence Lost National Initiative to address the growing problem of domestic sex trafficking of children in the United States.

http://www.fbi.gov/innolost/innolost.htm

International Parental Kidnapping

The FBI helps locate children who have been abducted by a parent and taken to parts unknown, often overseas. FBI field offices across the country serve as the primary point of contact for left-behind parents seeking help. To request assistance or learn more about the FBI's services, please contact the Crimes Against Children Coordinator at the local FBI office.

http://www.fbi.gov/hq/cid/cac/family.htm

RESOURCES

FBI Field Offices and Legal Attaches

Information about the FBI's field offices and legal attaches is available at:

www.fbi.gov

U.S. Department of Justice
Federal Bureau of Investigation

Innocent Images Unit

The Innocent Images Unit (IIU) maintains an embedded staff member at the National Center for Missing & Exploited Children (NCMEC) who addresses cyber tips; supports the Child Victim Identification Program; and serves as liaison to NCMEC personnel and to INTER-POL, EUROPOL, and all other Federal agency personnel who are also embedded at NCMEC.

Services offered in these fields:

- Technical assistance
- In-house training
- Out-of-house training
- Criminal investigation

Assistance provided in these areas:

- Child sexual exploitation
- Child pornography
- Internet crimes
- Crime prevention

Services provided to the following:

- Federal, State, and local agencies
- Community organizations
- General public

Contact Info

National Center for Missing & Exploited Children
699 Prince Street
Alexandria, VA 22314
tel 703–224–2150
fax 703–274–2121
email ecuassistance@ncmec.org

FBI/IIU PROGRAMS

Child Victim Identification Program

The FBI staff maintains the FBI Child Victim Identification Program and liaisons with NCMEC to assist agents with the timely review and identification of new and past victims. The staff assists the field with the submission of images and videos obtained through search warrants, knock and talks, and FBI Computer Analysis and Response Team (CART) digital forensic examinations. These reviews are the cornerstone of prosecutions as NCMEC maintains a database of law enforcement contacts for identified victims.

Cyber Tips

All cyber tips that are reported to NCMEC are reviewed for any intelligence that could be used to locate and secure a child from an exploitive environment. Information gathered on potential targets who are involved in the manufacture, distribution, transmission, and financial support of any image or movie of child exploitation is compiled and provided to FBI field divisions for further investigation.

FBI Safe Online Surfing (SOS) National Initiative

The FBI–SOS National Initiative is a collaborative effort with Nova Southeastern University. The FBI–SOS Internet Challenge, which is available at www.fbi-sos.org, is an interactive, online quiz designed to teach middle school students Internet safety. Each month a middle school is recognized as the "national winner" and awarded a trophy.

Innocent Images Intelligence

The Innocent Images Intelligence Unit provides a coordinated response to online crimes against children by collating and analyzing information obtained from all available sources. An embedded intelligence analyst assigned to work full-time at NCMEC reviews thousands of cyber tips every week to glean whatever intelligence is present and then disseminates that intelligence through proper channels. New applications are applied to existing criminal activities and, through a more coordinated approach, emerging threats are identified and proactively addressed.

www.fbi-sos.org

RESOURCES

FBI Resources

More information about IIU and the FBI's other resources is available at:

www.fbi.gov

U.S. Department of Justice
INTERPOL-Washington, U.S. National Central Bureau

INTERPOL is the international criminal police organization that is composed of designated national central bureaus (NCBs) in each of the 188 member nations. Each INTERPOL member country establishes, funds, and staffs a national central bureau, which serves as the point of contact for the international law enforcement community. Every NCB operates within the parameters of its own nation's laws and policies and within the framework of the INTERPOL constitution. In the United States, authority for the INTERPOL function rests with the Attorney General. Authority for administering the USNCB is shared by the Departments of Homeland Security and Justice.

USNCB's coordination services provide Federal, State, and local law enforcement authorities with the most effective means available to secure the assistance of foreign police in matters ranging from a criminal record check to the arrest and extradition of wanted persons.

Services offered in these fields:

- Receives foreign requests for criminal investigative assistance and directs those to the appropriate U.S. Federal, State, or local law enforcement or judicial authorities
- Receives domestic law enforcement requests and directs them to the appropriate NCB abroad
- Publishes INTERPOL international notices
- Enters information on a child-related crime, subject, victim, abducting parent, or missing child into the INTERPOL network
- Maintains list of INTERPOL State liaisons

Assistance provided in these areas:

- Parental abduction and kidnapping
- International abduction and kidnapping
- Runaway children
- Human trafficking
- Child sexual exploitation
- Child prostitution
- Sex tourism
- Internet crimes
- Tracking convicted sex offenders
- Apprehending non-compliant sex offenders

Services provided to the following:

- Federal, State, and local agencies
- INTERPOL member countries

Contact Info

Washington, U.S. National Central Bureau
(INTERPOL)
U.S. Department of Justice
Washington, DC 20530
tel 202–616–3900
fax 202–616–8400
NLETS DCINTER00
main Web site
www.usdoj.gov/usncb

INTERPOL–USNCB PROGRAMS

(see next page)

INTERPOL–USNCB PROGRAMS

Domestic Child Abduction Cases
In domestic child abduction cases, the initial request seeks to confirm if border-entry records can establish the presence of the abductor or the child in a foreign country. Once entry has been established, discreet verification is requested to confirm the exact location of the abductor in the hope of preventing that person from fleeing to another location.

If an NCB confirms the location of an offender, abductor, or child, USNCB notifies the originating police agency, which then coordinates subsequent investigative or retrieval efforts with the prosecuting attorney or the victim parent via the Department of State, Office of Children's Issues. If USNCB messages fail to locate an offender, abductor, or child, USNCB helps the originating agency complete the application process that will lead to publication of INTERPOL international notices.

Foreign Requests for Assistance
Foreign requests for investigative assistance are handled similarly to domestic cases. USNCB agents or analysts query various law enforcement databases—including the National Crime Information Center (NCIC)—to determine whether prior investigative information exists in the United States. The investigative request is then forwarded to the appropriate Federal or State police authority and oftentimes is coordinated with the National Center for Missing & Exploited Children. The results of such investigative actions are then routed back to USNCB for relay to the requesting country. If another NCB requests such action, USNCB can initiate a border-lookout notice using the Treasury Enforcement Communications System database and NCIC. Such a notice would request that INTERPOL be notified if the subject and/or missing/abducted child were to attempt to enter the United States.

RESOURCES

State Liaison Representatives
Contact INTERPOL for a list of State liaison representatives.

U.S. Department of Justice
Office of Justice Programs

Office for Victims of Crime

The mission of the Office for Victims of Crime (OVC) is to enhance the Nation's capacity to assist crime victims and to provide leadership in changing attitudes, policies, and practices in ways that will promote justice and healing for all victims.

OVC is charged by Congress with administering the Crime Victims Fund, a major source of funding for victim services throughout the Nation. Established by the Victims of Crime Act in 1984, the Fund supports thousands of programs annually that represent millions of dollars invested in victim compensation and assistance in every U.S. state and territory, as well as training and demonstration projects designed to enhance the skills of those who provide services to victims.

Each year, OVC funds programs that provide services, assistance, and resources to victims of crime, including child victims, in areas ranging from child sexual assault to international parental child abduction.

Services offered in these fields:

- Technical assistance
- Funding and grants

Assistance provided in these areas:

- International parental abduction and kidnapping
- Child sexual abuse
- Reference and referral resource information

Services provided to the following:

- Federal, State, and local agencies
- Community organizations

Contact Info

810 7th Street NW.
Washington, DC 20531

tel 202–307–5983

fax 202–305–2440

main Web site
www.ovc.gov

OVC PROGRAMS

Children's Justice Act Partnerships for Indian Communities Grant Program
Supported by the Crime Victims Fund, this grant program provides funding to assist American Indian/Alaska native communities in developing, establishing, and operating programs to improve the investigation and prosecution of child abuse, including child sexual abuse. Specialized services aim to minimize trauma by tailoring standard procedures to more sensitively respond to child victims.

Victim Reunification Travel Program

This program provides funding to help left-behind parents in international child abduction cases. Support under this program is provided via an intra-agency authorization with the Office of Juvenile Justice and Delinquency Prevention (OJJDP) and an OJJDP grant to the National Center for Missing & Exploited Children.

OVC Web site

OVC's main Web site provides publications, resource links, answers to frequently asked questions, and funding information in the areas of child victimization, or the more specialized subjects of "Missing and Exploited Children" or "Parental Kidnapping" in the Crime Victimization section of the site.

www.ovc.gov

RESOURCES

OVC is dedicated to continuously improving the national response to crime victims by enhancing the skills and abilities of victim service providers, and informing and educating a variety of audiences on numerous subjects of specific interest, including information on assisting child victims who have been exposed to physical or emotional abuse in the home, school, or community or who have witnessed crime or family violence.

OVC Online Directory of Crime Victim Services

The Online Directory lists **nonemergency** victim services organizations that provide assistance to victims of crime, including child victims, in the United States and abroad.

www.ovc.gov

OVC Training and Technical Assistance Center

The Training and Technical Assistance Center is OVC's main source of up-to-date information about training courses and workshops focusing on victims of crime, including child victims, from easily accessible online curriculums such as Victim Assistance Training (VAT) Online to workshops regularly held at locations across the country.

www.ovcttac.gov

U.S. Department of Justice
Office of Justice Programs
Office of Juvenile Justice and Delinquency Prevention
Child Protection Division

In 2000, the Office of Juvenile Justice and Delinquency Prevention (OJJDP) created the Child Protection Division (CPD) to oversee its efforts to protect children from violence, abuse, neglect, and other forms of victimization. CPD administers all programs related to crimes against children, including Internet crimes and commercial sexual exploitation of children; provides leadership and funding in the areas of prevention, intervention, treatment, and enforcement; and promotes the effective use of policies and procedures to address the problems of missing, neglected, abused, and exploited children. CPD conducts research, demonstration, and service programs; provides training and technical assistance; provides assistance and support to the Association of Missing and Exploited Children's Organizations, the National Center for Missing & Exploited Children, and Team H.O.P.E. (Help Offering Parents Empowerment); and works closely with the National AMBER (America's Missing: Broadcast Emergency Response) Alert coordinator to support the development and improvement of the AMBER Alert system nationwide.

Since 1984, training and technical assistance have been provided to local law enforcement agencies to aid in their efforts to locate and recover missing children. Each year CPD trains more than 4,500 law enforcement officials in the investigation of missing children cases, at no cost to State or local governments.

Services offered in these fields:

• Program development and implementation

• Funding and grants

Assistance provided in these areas:

• Child abduction

• Child sexual exploitation

• Child prostitution

• Child pornography

• Internet crimes

Services provided to the following:

• Federal, State, and local agencies

• Community organizations

• Legislative and policy groups

• General public

Contact Info
810 7th Street NW.
Washington, DC 20531

tel 202–307–5911

main Web site
www.ojjdp.gov

OJJDP/CPD PROGRAMS

(see next page)

OJJDP/CPD PROGRAMS

AMBER Alert Training and Technical Assistance Program

Training and technical assistance are available to communities and jurisdictions interested in developing and/or enhancing their AMBER Alert programs. AMBER Alert coordinators are also available.

www.ojp.usdoj.gov/amberalert/home.html

Protecting Children Online

This program enhances law enforcement's ability to investigate computer crimes against children.

http://dept.fvtc.edu/childprotectiontraining

Protecting Children Online for Prosecutors

This program provides prosecutors with the information they need to understand, recognize, and prosecute computer crimes against children.

http://dept.fvtc.edu/childprotectiontraining

School Resource Officer Leadership Program

This program demonstrates standards of excellence and best practices in the enhanced role of the school resource officer as a leader in planning and maintaining a safe school environment.

http://dept.fvtc.edu/childprotectiontraining

Team Investigative Process for Missing, Abused, and Exploited Children

This intensive team-training program promotes the development of a community-based, interdisciplinary team process for effectively investigating cases involving missing, abused, and exploited children.

http://dept.fvtc.edu/childprotectiontraining

CONFERENCES, WORKSHOPS, AND TRAININGS

Child Abuse and Exploitation Investigative Techniques

This course enhances the skills of experienced law enforcement officials and other professionals who investigate cases involving child abuse, sexual exploitation of children, child pornography, and missing children.

http://dept.fvtc.edu/childprotectiontraining

Child Fatality Investigations

This course provides law enforcement officers, child protective service workers, medical personnel, and other professionals with comprehensive training on the detection, intervention, investigation, and prosecution of cases involving fatal child abuse and neglect.

http://dept.fvtc.edu/childprotectiontraining

Child Sexual Exploitation Investigations

This course provides law enforcement officials and other professionals with the information they need to understand, recognize, investigate, and resolve cases of child pornography and sexual exploitation.

http://dept.fvtc.edu/childprotectiontraining

Internet Crimes Against Children Task Force Training

Training is available to help State and local law enforcement with the complex and challenging investigations related to Internet crimes. Information about these training opportunities, which are available at little or no cost to law enforcement agencies, is available at:

www.icactraining.org

Responding to Missing and Abducted Children

This course enhances the knowledge and skills of law enforcement officials who investigate cases involving abducted, runaway, and other missing youth.

http://dept.fvtc.edu/childprotectiontraining

RESOURCES

Training, Programs, and Publications

http://www.ojjdp.ncjrs.gov/
http://www.ncjrs.gov/
301–519–5500
1–800–851–3420

U.S. Department of State
Bureau of Consular Affairs
Office of Children's Issues

The Office of Children's Issues (CI) plays an active role in responding to and preventing international parental child abduction. CI serves as the U.S. Central Authority for the 1980 Hague Convention on the Civil Aspects of International Child Abduction. The agency aims to prevent and resolve cases through the Hague Abduction Convention, coordination with law enforcement, and other legal methods. By partnering with U.S. embassies and consulates, CI conducts diplomatic efforts to improve cooperation between the United States and other nations on countering international parental child abduction.

Services offered in these fields:

- Technical assistance
- In-house training
- Out-of-house training
- Program development and implementation
- Research and program evaluation
- Case management support
- Hague application processing
- Central Authority duties

Assistance provided in these areas:

- Child abduction
- Parental abduction and kidnapping
- Crime prevention
- International adoption

Services provided to the following:

- Federal, State, and local agencies
- Community organizations
- Legislative and policy groups
- Children and families, regardless of citizenship; attorneys and judges; law enforcement agencies; nongovernmental organizations; and other stakeholders
- General public

Contact Info

2201 C Street NW.
SA-29, Fourth Floor
Washington, DC 20520
tel 888–407–4747
fax 202–736–9133
email AbductionUSCA@state.gov
main Web site
www.Trave .State.gov/ch dabduct on

CI PROGRAMS

Children's Passport Issuance Alert Program
The Children's Passport Issuance Alert Program is an important tool for preventing international parental child abduction. The program allows parents to register their U.S. citizen children in the Department's Passport Lookout System. The Passport Lookout System gives all domestic passport agencies and U.S. embassies and consulates abroad an alert on a child's name if a parent or guardian registers an objection to passport issuance for his or her child. If a passport application is submitted for a child who is registered in the program, the Department alerts the parent(s). This provides

parents advance warning of possible plans for international travel with the child.

PreventAbduction@state.gov
www.travel.state.gov/abduction/abduction
_580.html

RESOURCES

Annual Report to Congress on Compliance with the Hague Abduction Convention

www.travel.state.gov/abduction/resources/
congressreport/congressreport_4308.html

U.S. Postal Service
U.S. Postal Inspection Service

The U.S. Postal Inspection Service (USPIS) is the Federal law enforcement arm of the U.S. Postal Service with responsibility for investigating crimes involving all child pornography and child sexual exploitation offenses. The USPIS was the first Federal law enforcement agency to aggressively identify, target, and arrest those who produce and traffic in child pornography. Postal inspectors focus their investigations on commercial mail distributors of child pornography and their customers. In addition, postal inspectors target individuals who use the mail to distribute, receive, trade, buy, or advertise child pornography.

Services offered in these fields:

- Technical assistance
- Address checks
- Criminal investigation

Assistance provided in these areas:

- Parental abduction and kidnapping
- Child sexual exploitation
- Child pornography
- Internet crimes

Services provided to the following:

- Federal, State, and local agencies

Contact Info

Criminal Investigations
475 L'Enfant Plaza SW.
Washington, DC 20260

tel 202–268–4498

fax 202–268–6532

main Web site
https://postalinspectors.uspis.gov/

USPIS PROGRAMS

Prohibited Mailings, Child Exploitation Program

Postal inspectors have established a nationwide network of intelligence, incorporating a wide variety of mail-based undercover programs designed to identify suspects and develop prosecutable cases. In addition, the USPIS works with the Department of Justice's Child Exploitation and Obscenity Section (DOJ/CEOS) and all U.S. attorney's offices across the United States to investigate child sexual exploitation involving the U.S. mail.

Deliver Me Home

The USPIS partners with the National Center for Missing & Exploited Children (NCMEC) and the Postal Service to disseminate posters of missing children via mail carriers to every household in designated zip codes.

RESOURCES

The USPIS has both full-time and part-time child exploitation specialists located across the United States. In addition, the USPIS has one full-time postal inspector assigned to DOJ/CEOS in Washington, DC, and one full-time postal inspector assigned to NCMEC in Alexandria, VA. To reach the most recently assigned postal inspector for a specific location, contact the National Child Pornography Program Manager.

Non-Federal Agencies

Association of Missing and Exploited Children's Organizations, Inc.

The Association of Missing and Exploited Children's Organizations, Inc. (AMECO), is an association of nonprofit organizations that assist in the prevention, recovery, and reintegration of missing children. AMECO builds and nurtures credible, ethical, and effective nonprofit organizations that serve missing and exploited children and their families as well as law enforcement.

Services offered in these fields:

- Technical assistance
- In-house training
- Out-of-house training
- Networking opportunities
- Public education

Assistance provided in these areas:

- Reference and referral resource information
- Nonprofit development

Services provided to the following:

- Nonprofit member organizations

Contact Info

P.O. Box 320338
Alexandria, VA 22320

tel 703–838–8379

fax 877–839–8279

email info@amecoinc.org

CONFERENCES, WORKSHOPS, AND TRAINING

Training Conferences
Biannual training conferences provide a platform for AMECO members to discuss and share best practices with one another. The fall conference, which is sponsored by NCMEC and OJJDP, includes State clearinghouses.

RESOURCES

AMECO Member Organizations and State Clearinghouses

www.amecoinc.org

AMECO Member Organizations

- Technical assistance
- Information dissemination and awareness raising
- Public education

- Victim reunification
- Child abduction
- Parental abduction and kidnapping
- International abduction and kidnapping
- Runaway children
- Child sexual exploitation
- Child pornography
- Internet crimes
- Reference and referral resource information

- Federal, State, and local agencies
- Community organizations
- Legislative and policy groups
- General public

National Center for Missing & Exploited Children®

Services offered in these fields:

- Technical assistance to families and professionals
- In-house training
- Out-of-house training
- Onsite technical assistance
- Program development and implementation
- Publication support
- Public education
- Family support

Assistance provided in these areas:

- Child abduction
- Parental abduction and kidnapping
- Victim reunification
- Runaway children
- Child sexual exploitation
- Child prostitution
- Child pornography
- Sex tourism
- Internet crimes committed against children
- Forensic sciences
- Crime prevention
- Reference and referral resource information

Services provided to the following:

- Federal, State, and local agencies
- Community organizations
- Policy groups
- Victim families
- General public

The National Center for Missing & Exploited Children (NCMEC) serves as the national resource center and information clearinghouse for missing and sexually exploited children. The agency works to find missing children, eliminate child sexual exploitation, and prevent child victimization.

Contact Info

Charles B. Wang International
  Children's Building
699 Prince Street
Alexandria, VA 22314–3175

tel 1–800–THE–LOST®
  (1–800–843–5678)

tdd 1–800–826–7653

fax 703–224–2122

email resources@ncmec.org

NCMEC PROGRAMS

Call Center

The NCMEC Call Center receives toll-free calls from the United States, Canada, Mexico, and many other countries on its telephone hotline (1–800–THE–LOST, 1–800–843–5678). Specially trained staff members record lead and sighting information, help both family members and professionals in their search for missing children, assist sexually exploited children and their families, work with hearing impaired callers through the NCMEC TDD line, process requests from families with travel reunification needs, offer direct after-hours assistance to law enforcement, and provide safety information to help prevent the abduction and sexual exploitation of children. NCMEC is able to facilitate communication with callers in 180 different languages.

Case Analysis Division

The Case Analysis Division provides analytical support to missing and abducted children investigations. Staff members assess all leads and sightings, evaluate each lead for its potential usefulness, add value to leads by providing the most current and relevant information available, and disseminate that information to the appropriate law enforcement agencies. NCMEC facilitates provision for up-to-date national sex offender information to provide rapid data about the geographical proximity of these subjects to both new and unresolved cases of significance and relevance.

Sex Offender Tracking. NCMEC serves as an information clearinghouse for law enforcement agencies in their efforts to locate noncompliant, absconded, registered sex offenders by providing technical assistance and access to NCMEC databases, external sources, and geographic databases.

www.missingkids.com

CyberTipline

NCMEC operates this congressionally mandated reporting Web site for child sexual exploitation, including child pornography and online enticement.

http://www.cybertipline.com

Exploited Children Division

The Exploited Children Division serves as a resource for families, law enforcement agencies, and members of the public on the sexual exploitation of children. Analysts process information reported to the CyberTipline; disseminate leads; and provide technical assistance to local, State, Federal, and international law enforcement agencies investigating cases involving the sexual exploitation of children.

Child Victim Identification Program. NCMEC serves as the clearinghouse in the United States for cases involving child pornography and as the main point of contact for international agencies seeking to identify victims.

www.cybertipline.com

Family Advocacy Division

The Family Advocacy Division provides technical assistance, referrals, and crisis intervention services for families, law enforcement officials, and family advocacy agencies.

Child Safety: Education and Prevention Materials. NCMEC's publications and other educational materials can be ordered by calling NCMEC or downloaded online.

Family Reunification Assistance. NCMEC arranges free transportation for families who meet eligibility requirements to reunite with their children. This service is made possible through the U.S. Department of Justice's Office for Victims of Crime and NCMEC's private sector transportation partners, including American Airlines, Amtrak, Continental Airlines, and Greyhound Lines.

Missing Children Division

The Missing Children Division works with law enforcement agencies and with the families of missing and abducted children to provide technical assistance and all available search resources. Staff members maintain up-to-date case information, establish regular contact with both families and investigative agencies, certify and prepare posters for dissemination, and post updates of each child's information on NCMEC's Web site.

AMBER Alert. NCMEC assists the Assistant Attorney General within the U.S. Department of Justice's Office of Justice Programs with AMBER Alert activations and disseminates AMBER Alert messages to secondary communications distributors.

Family Abduction. NCMEC helps families, law enforcement agencies, attorneys, and others find and recover children who are the victims of family abduction.

www.missingkids.com

Forensic Assistance. NCMEC provides age-progressed photographs of missing children; creates reconstructed facial images of unidentified deceased children; and helps families, law enforcement agencies, and medical examiners resolve long-term missing children cases.

Infant Abduction Prevention Program. NCMEC provides infant abduction prevention training to nursing associations, hospital security associations, and law enforcement agencies as well as investigative assistance to law enforcement in infant abduction cases.

Photo and Poster Distribution. Through a network of nearly 400 active private sector partners, NCMEC has distributed more than half a million photographs of missing children. NCMEC coordinates national media exposure of missing children cases through its partnership with major television networks, leading nationwide publishers, and major corporations. NCMEC also has "broadcast" fax capabilities that provide rapid dissemination of vital information concerning missing and abducted children to key locations throughout the country.

Project ALERT. Project ALERT (America's Law Enforcement Retiree Team) is comprised of skilled, retired law enforcement officers who specialize in long-term missing child cases. Team members provide free onsite assistance to law enforcement.

Team Adam. Team Adam sends experienced investigative specialists to the sites of serious and emerging child abductions, missing child incidents, and cases involving child sexual exploitation to advise local investigators.

CONFERENCES, WORKSHOPS, AND TRAININGS
E-mail jrletc@ncmec.org for course calendars

Missing and Exploited Children Chief Executive Officer Seminar
This 2-day seminar orients police chiefs and sheriffs to issues related to missing and sexually exploited children.

Protecting Children Online
This 4½-day seminar familiarizes law enforcement investigators with the technical and legal issues surrounding investigations of computer-facilitated crimes committed against children.

Protecting Children Online for Prosecutors
This 4½-day seminar for prosecutors discusses the ever-evolving legal and technical issues surrounding investigations of computer-facilitated crimes committed against children.

Protecting Children Online: Unit Commander/Policy Training
This 2½-day seminar familiarizes law enforcement supervisors with the legal, technical, and management issues underlying investigations of computer-facilitated crimes committed against children.

Responding to Missing and Abducted Children
This 4½-day seminar equips law enforcement to properly understand, investigate, and resolve missing and abducted children cases.

RESOURCES

State Clearinghouses

http://www.missingkids.com

Index

Index

Assistance provided in these areas:	CB/OCAN	CEOS	CI	DOD	FALET	FBI/CACU	FBI/IIU	FYSB	ICE	INTERPOL-USNCB	OJJDP/CPD	OSDFS	OVC	USPIS	USSS	AMECO	NCMEC
Apprehending non-compliant sex offenders										•							
Child abduction		•	•	•	•					•							•
Child pornography		•			•	•			•	•				•	•		•
Child prostitution		•			•	•	•		•	•							
Child sexual abuse											•						
Child sexual exploitation	•	•			•	•	•	•	•	•		•					
Child welfare	•																
Crime prevention			•			•	•										•
Crime victim compensation													•				
Forensic sciences					•				•	•					•		
Human trafficking					•	•			•	•	•						
International abduction and kidnapping					•	•				•							
International adoption	•																
International parental abduction and kidnapping	•										•						
Internet crimes					•	•		•	•	•	•	•		•	•		
Internet crimes against children	•																•
Military resources				•													
Nonprofit development																•	
Parental abduction and kidnapping		•	•		•				•					•			•
Reference and referral resource information						•		•						•	•	•	•
Runaway children					•	•		•	•								•
Sex tourism		•	•		•				•	•							•
Teen dating violence								•				•					
Tracking convicted sex offenders										•							
Victim reunification																•	•

Index

Notes

www.ingramcontent.com/pod-product-compliance
Lightning Source LLC
Chambersburg PA
CBHW071637170526
45166CB00003B/1352